carrie underwood
CARNIVAL RIDE

Management Simon Fuller, Ann Edelblute; 19 Management. A 19 Entertainment Production.
Album Art Direction S Wade Hunt *Album Design* Astrid Herbold May
Album Notes/Creative Production Judy Forde-Blair
A&R Direction Renée Bell
Photography Andrew Eccles
Hair/Makeup Melissa Schleicher
Stylist Trish Townsend

Alfred

Alfred Publishing Co., Inc.
16320 Roscoe Blvd., Suite 100
P.O. Box 10003
Van Nuys, CA 91410-0003
alfred.com

ISBN-10: 0-7390-5104-0
ISBN-13: 978-0-7390-5104-7

FLAT ON THE FLOOR

Words and Music by
BRETT JAMES and ASHLEY MONROE

Moderate two-beat ($\downarrow$ = 88)

12

All-American Girl

Words and Music by
CARRIE UNDERWOOD, KELLIE LOVELACE
and ASHLEY GORLEY

Verse:

1. Since the day they___ got mar - ried,___ he'd been pray - in' for a
2. Six - teen short___ years lat - er,___ she was fall - in' for the

All-American Girl - 6 - 1
29218

lit - tle__ ba - by__ boy._____
se - nior__ foot - ball__ star._____

Some - one he could take fish - in',____
Be - fore you knew it, he was drop - pin' pass - es,____

throw the foot - ball and be__ his pride_ and__ joy.____
skip - pin' prac - tice just to spend more time__ with__ her.____

He could al - read - y see him
The coach said,__ "Hey, son,

SO SMALL

Words and Music by
CARRIE UNDERWOOD, HILLARY LINDSEY
and LUKE LAIRD

So Small - 8 - 1
29218

22

sit-tin' 'round think-in' 'bout what you can't change and wor - ry-ing a - bout_ all the wrong things,_ time's_

_ fly-in' by,_ mov-in' so fast._ You bet - ter make it count, 'cause you can't get it back. Some -

Chorus:

times_ that moun - tain you've_ been climb - in' is just a grain_ of_ sand._

_

And what

yeah, yeah, yeah, yeah._____ 'Cause some -

times_____ that moun - tain you've_ been climb - ing is just a grain_ of_____

____ sand._____ And what

you've been out_ there search - ing for for - ev - er is in_____ your___

JUST A DREAM

Words and Music by
HILLARY LINDSEY, STEVE McEWAN
and GORDIE SAMPSON

Moderately slow ♩ = 72

Em7　　　G　　　Em7　　　G

(with pedal)

mf

Verse:

Em　　　　　　　　　　　　　　G

two weeks af-ter the day___ she turned___ eigh-teen,___ all___ dressed___ in white,___
preach-er man said, "Let us bow___ our heads___ and pray.___ Lord, please lift his soul___

Em　　　　　　　　　　　　　　G

___ go-in' to the church that night.___ She had his
and heal this hurt."___ Then the

GET OUT OF THIS TOWN

Words and Music by
HILLARY LINDSEY, STEVE McEWAN
and GORDIE SAMPSON

Moderate rock (♩ = 136)

1. Got it

Verses 1 & 2:

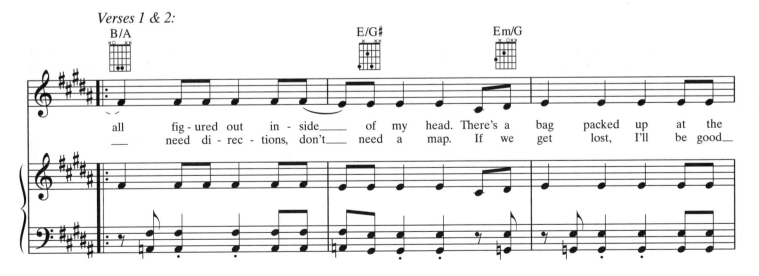

all fig-ured out in-side____ of my head. There's a bag packed up at the
___ need di-rec-tions, don't____ need a map. If we get lost, I'll be good____

Get Out of This Town - 5 - 1
29218

CRAZY DREAMS

Words and Music by
CARRIE UNDERWOOD, TROY VERGES
and BARRY DEAN

Moderately ♩ = 92

*Original recording in F♯ major. Guitar is tuned down 1/2 step.

Crazy Dreams - 8 - 1
29218

Chorus 1:

Verse:

yeah.

C

Em7

D

...end solo)

Chorus 3:

G5

3. I've met some go - get - ters, some dif - f'rence mak - ers,

C

small town he - roes and big chance tak - ers. I've met some young hearts

Chorus 4:

I KNOW YOU WON'T

Words and Music by
WENDELL MOBLEY, STEVE McEWAN
and NEIL THRASHER

LAST NAME

50

Gtr. tuned down 1/2 step:
⑥ = E♭ ③ = G♭
⑤ = A♭ ② = B♭
④ = D♭ ① = E♭

Moderately slow country rock ♩ = 80 (♫ = ♪ ♪)

Words and Music by
CARRIE UNDERWOOD, HILLARY LINDSEY
and LUKE LAIRD

Verses 1 & 2:

1. Last night, I got served a lit-tle bit too much of that poi-son, ba - by.
2. We left the club right a-round three o'-clock in the morn - ing. His

Last night, I did things I'm not proud of, and I got a lit-tle cra - zy.
Pin - to sit-tin' there in the park-ing lot, well, it should-'ve been a warn - ing.

Last Name - 8 - 1
29218

53

Last Name - 8 - 4
29218

YOU WON'T FIND THIS

Verse 2:
Now there's once in a lifetime
And there's once in a while.
And the difference between the two
Is about a million miles.
Oh, you might get lucky
While the moon is looking on,
But in the truth of the morning,
The stars will be long gone.
(To Chorus:)

I TOLD YOU SO

Words and Music by
RANDY TRAVIS

THE MORE BOYS I MEET

Words and Music by
STEVE McEWAN and GORDON KENNEDY

Moderately, with a strong beat ♩ = 126

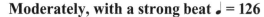

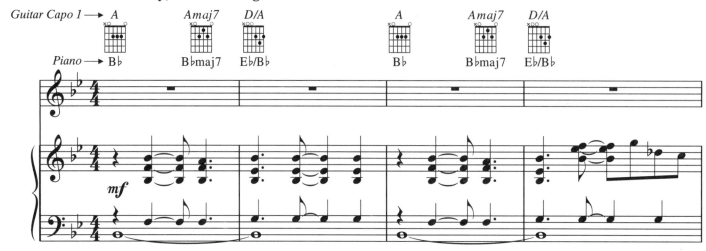

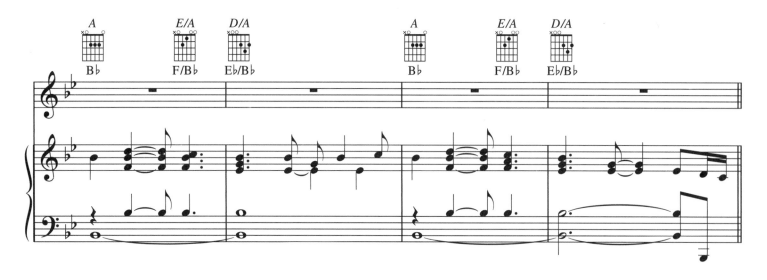

Verse 1:

1. This boy here wants to move too__ fast.__ He see's__ my fu - ture__ as

The More Boys I Meet - 6 - 1
29218

TWISTED

Words and Music by
HILLARY LINDSEY, BRETT JAMES
and LUKE LAIRD

WHEEL OF THE WORLD

Words and Music by
HILLARY LINDSEY, CHRIS LINDSEY
and AIMEE MAYO

Moderately slow ♩ = 96

Verse 2:

turn-ing a-round___ and a-round._____ 2. God put us here___

on this car-ni-val ride;_____ we close our eyes,_____ nev-er know-ing where___

___ it-'ll take___ us next.___ Ba-bies are born,___ and at the same time,___

_____ some-one's tak-ing their___ last breath._____ It's the wheel___